MEL BAY PRESENTS

Mandolin Tune Book

POCKETBOOK DELUXE SERIES
by William Bay

G000018023

Visit us on the Web at www.melbay.com — E-mail us at email@melbay.com

Table of Contents

Blackberry Blossom

St. Clair's Hornpipe

St. Anne's Reel

The Teetotaller's Reel

Whiskey Before Breakfast

Morrison's Jig

Irish Jig

Billy in the Low Ground

Swallowtail Jig

Irish Jig

Bill Cheatham

Blessed Quietness
(Gospel Song)

Soppin' the Gravy

Gladiator Reel

Cold, Frosty Morning

Lost Indian

Red Fox Waltz

Brush Creek

William Bay

Young McGoldrick

William Bay

The Downfall of Paris

Set Dance

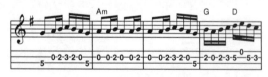

Bennett's Favorite Reel 21

Winfield Waltz

William Bay

Drowsy Maggie

An Comhra Donn

Hornpipe

Luckie Bawdins' Reel

Scottish

Far from Home

Shetland Islands Reel

Lark in the Morning

Lady's Fancy

Buttermilk Jig

Eleven Mile Canyon

William Bay

Star of Bethlehem

Caleb's Gorge

William Bay

34 Witch of the Wave Reel

Cumberland Ridge

William Bay

35

Reel De Lapin

French Canadian

My Irish Home

William Bay

Dixie Breakdown

Neapolitan Threshers

Jig

Red Haired Boy

Harvest Moon Strathspey

Southwind Waltz

Mere Point

William Bay

43

44

Morning Glory

William Bay

Emerald Shores

William Bay

The Rights of Man

Stone's Rag

Swing Feeling

American Rag

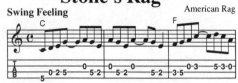

Silver Bell

Bacon in the Skillet

William Bay

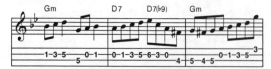

Silverheel's Shuffle

William Bay

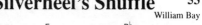

Sundance

William Bay

The Promenade

William Bay

Obadiah Johnson

William Bay

Midnight Flight

William Bay

High Five

William Bay

Soulard

William Bay

Lively Tempo

The Hallelujah Side

Precious Memories

Leaning on the
Everlasting Arms

Living Where the Healing Waters Flow

Only Trust Him

I Am Resolved

66 I Need Thee Every Hour

Standing on the Promises

The Solid Rock

Lord, I'm Coming Home

Lily of the Valley

Blessed Assurance

There is a Fountain

Heavenly Father
We Appreciate You

⁷⁴ There is Glory in my Soul

Flowers of Sweet Erin the Green

Crazy Creek

Ivy Leaf Reel

Bull Durham

William Bay

Old Pail

William Bay

Opening Day

William Bay

The Red Hen

William Bay

Kirkwood Klucker

William Bay

High Steppin'

Willam Bay

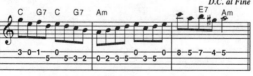

Steep Levee

William Bay

Stuck in the Kitchen

William Bay

Running Naked Through the Briar Patch

William Bay

D.C. al Fine

Riley McGurk

William Bay

Brass Buttons

William Bay

D.C. al Fine

Bucharest

William Bay

Levelland by Night

William Bay

Canadian Bacon

William Bay

Frost on the Meadow

William Bay

Snowflakes

William Bay

Rise 'n Shine

William Bay